Sedimentary Rocks

by Melissa Stewart

Heinemann Library
CHICAGO, ILLINOIS

Designed by Ox and Company

An Editorial Directions book

Printed in China

06 05 04 03
10 9 8 7 6 5 4 3 2

Library of Congress Cataloging-in-Publication Data
Stewart, Melissa.
    Sedimentary rocks / Melissa Stewart.
        p. cm.—(Rocks and minerals)
Includes bibliographical references and index.
Summary: Provides an overview of sedimentary rocks, discussing their formation,
location, identifying characteristics, history, significance, and uses throughout
the world.
    ISBN: 1-58810-259-9 (HC), 1-4034-0095-4 (Pbk.)
    1. Rocks, Sedimentary—Juvenile literature. [1. Rocks, Sedimentary.] I. Title.
QE471 .S68 2002
552'.5—dc21
                                                    2001002760

Acknowledgments
The author and publishers are grateful to the following for permission to reproduce copyright material:

Photographs ©: Cover background, EyeWire; cover foreground, David Johnson/Reed Consumer Books, Ltd.; p. 4 top, Jeffrey
Meyers/Frozen Images/The Image Works; p. 4 bottom, Ric Ergenbright/Corbis; p. 5, Ann & Rob Simpson/Simpson's Nature
Photography; p. 8 top, Ross Frid/Visuals Unlimited, Inc; p. 8 bottom, Sharon Gerig/Tom Stack & Associates; p. 9, Doug
Sokell/Tom Stack & Associates; p. 10, Sven Martson/The Image Works; p. 11, NASA/TSADO/Tom Stack & Associates;
p. 13, A.J. Copley/Visuals Unlimited, Inc.; p. 14, Tom Bean; p. 15, Grace Davies Photography; p. 16, Adam Woolfitt/Corbis; p.
17, Charles & Judy Walker/Liaison International/Hulton Archive; p. 18, James P. Rowan; p. 19, Grace Davies Photography; p.
21, Judyth Platt/Ecoscene/Corbis; p. 22, Gianni Dagli Orti/Corbis; p. 23, Mike Okoniewski/Gamma Liaison/Hulton Archive;
p. 24, James P. Rowan; pp. 25, 26, Tom Bean; p. 27, Jonathan Blair/Corbis; pp. 28, 29, B. Daemmrich/The Image Works.

Some words are shown in bold, **like this.** You can find out what they mean by looking in the glossary.

Contents

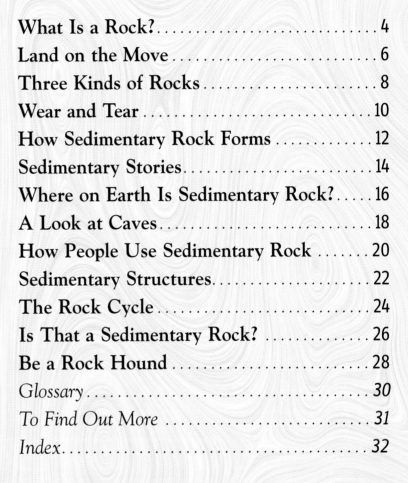

What Is a Rock?

Take a look around your classroom at school. How many kinds of rock do you see? Chalk is made from rock, and so is the concrete in the walls and the glass in the windows. The paper you write on was made from trees, but it also contains a little bit of ground-up rock. You probably don't pay much attention to the rocks around you, but maybe you should. Every rock has a story to tell.

Are you surprised to hear that chalk is made of rock? Chalk is made of limestone, a sedimentary rock formed by the shells and skeletons of sea animals.

Chalk, concrete, glass, and paper all contain sedimentary rock. Sedimentary rock is one of three kinds of rocks found in the world. The other

Rocks come in all shapes and sizes. The chalky White Cliffs of Dover (right) along the southeastern coast of England are a mountain–sized chunk of sedimentary rock made of minerals from seashells.

two kinds are **igneous rock** and **metamorphic rock.** Each kind of rock forms in a different way, but all rocks are made of **minerals.**

A mineral is a natural solid material. No matter where you find it, a mineral always has the same chemical makeup and the same structure. In other words, the **atoms** that mix together to form a mineral always arrange themselves in the same way. Most minerals have a **crystal** structure. Crystals usually have a regular shape and smooth, flat sides called **faces.**

Limestone is a sedimentary rock that usually contains minerals of calcite, dolomite, and aragonite. The crystal structure of calcite is made up of calcium, carbon, and oxygen atoms that are always arranged in the same way. A crystal of calcite always has six faces.

These limestone cliffs in a Virginia river valley are made mostly of calcite. Pure calcite is clear or white, but other minerals in limestone give it color.

Land on the Move

Sedimentary rock is the most common kind of rock on Earth's surface. But just a few miles underground, Earth's makeup changes. Below Earth's solid **crust** is the **mantle**—a layer of hot, liquid rock called **magma.** The mantle surrounds Earth's central **core.** The outer core is made of melted metals, but the inner core is solid.

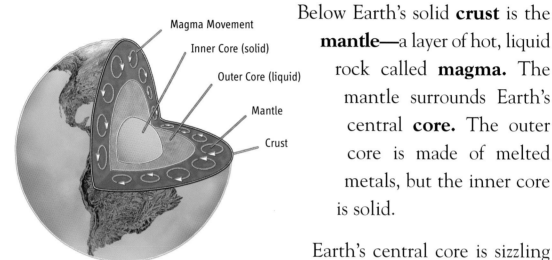

Magma Movement

Inner Core (solid)

Outer Core (liquid)

Mantle

Crust

The thin outer layer of Earth is the crust. The next layer, the mantle, is made of magma that is constantly moving. The core is made of an outer liquid core and an inner solid core.

Earth's central core is sizzling hot—more than 9,000 degrees Fahrenheit (5,000 degrees Celsius). As heat from the solid metallic core escapes first into the liquid outer core and then into the mantle, it pushes magma toward the surface. Meanwhile, cooler magma at the top of the mantle moves down to take its place. Over millions of years, magma slowly circles through Earth's mantle.

Earth's crust is made up of giant slabs of rock called **plates.** These plates fit together like the pieces of a jigsaw puzzle. As magma swirls within the mantle, the plates move too. Over time, this

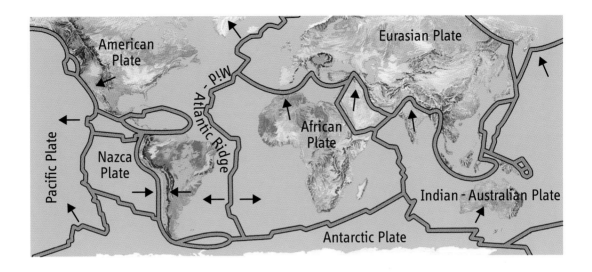

process reshapes the land and moves it from place to place.

Scientists believe that Earth formed about 4.6 billion years ago, but it has looked the way it does today for only about 65 million years. Before that, the continents were in different places. About 1.1 billion years ago, Earth had one large continent called Rodinia. The center of Rodinia was close to the South Pole.

Then, about 600 million years ago, Rodinia broke into three large pieces, and most of the land drifted north. Nearly 180 million years ago, all of Earth's land formed a second giant continent called Pangaea. As time passed, the plates continued to travel across Earth's surface to form the continents we know today—and they are still on the move. Perhaps, one day, all of Earth's land will come together again and form a third giant continent.

Earth's surface is broken into many plates. The major plates are labeled on this diagram. The plates are moving constantly, though very slowly, in the direction of the arrows. The Mid-Atlantic Ridge is a rift formed by two plates moving apart.

Three Kinds of Rocks

Earth has three kinds of rocks—sedimentary, **igneous,** and **metamorphic.** Each kind of rock forms in a different way. Sedimentary rock is made of layers of mud, clay, and sand that have been compressed and stuck together over time. Limestone, shale, graywacke, siltstone, sandstone, breccia, chert, flint, and rock salt are all examples of sedimentary rock.

Igneous rock forms when **magma** from Earth's **mantle** cools and hardens. Sometimes the magma forces its way up to Earth's surface and spills onto the land through a **volcano.** Over time, large volcanic mountains of igneous rock pile up. This kind of igneous rock cools quickly and has very small **crystals.** In other cases, pools of magma become trapped at the top of the mantle and cool slowly

Shale (above) is a sedimentary rock formed by layers of clay and mud. It feels smooth and greasy and is soft enough to scratch. Basalt (below) is a kind of igneous rock. It forms when lava cools and hardens.

over thousands of years. Some of the largest and most beautiful crystals in the world were formed in this way. Granite, gabbro, basalt, and obsidian are examples of igneous rock.

Metamorphic rock forms when heat or pressure changes the **minerals** within sedimentary rock, igneous rock, or another metamorphic rock. This often happens when Earth's **plates** collide and push up tall mountain ranges. Metamorphic rock also forms when a stream of magma bursts into the **crust** and cooks the surrounding rock. Marble, slate, and gneiss are examples of metamorphic rock.

Gneiss is a metamorphic rock. The beautiful bands that run through it form as granite or schist is heated, twisted, and squeezed deep under the ground.

WHAT A DISCOVERY!

In 1785, a Scottish doctor named James Hutton noticed layers of sedimentary rock in a riverbank near his home. At that time, most scientists thought Earth was about 6,000 years old. But Hutton thought it must have taken much longer for these layers of rock to build up. He suggested that Earth might be more than a million years old. Many scientists laughed at Hutton's theory, but today we know that Earth is about 4.6 billion years old.

9

Wear and Tear

As this tree grows around a large rock, the rock slowly undergoes weathering. On the ground, you can see pieces that have already broken off.

Have you ever heard a friend say something is "as hard as a rock"? Rocks are so hard that they may seem indestructible. But under the right conditions, wind and water are even tougher than rock. Over time, the force of crashing ocean waves, fast-flowing streams, whipping winds, and gigantic glaciers can slowly wear away, or **erode,** even the hardest rock.

Rocks can also be broken down by a process called **weathering.** In places with hot days and cool nights, rock expands and shrinks over and over.

DID YOU KNOW?

Sedimentary rock erodes and weathers more quickly than other kinds of rock because it is softer and is arranged in layers that often break apart easily.

Eventually, the rock weakens and crumbles. In addition, when water flows into a rock's nooks and crannies and then freezes, the rock may shatter. Plant roots can grow into cracks in rocks and slowly split them apart. **Acid rain** and snow are also tough enough to destroy rock. So are chemicals released by some tiny creatures that live in the soil.

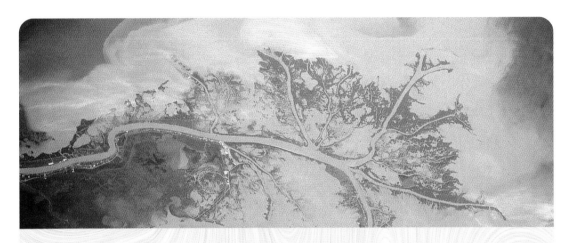

THE POWER OF WATER

Are you surprised that water—that clear liquid you drink every day—has the power to break down most of the world's rocks? Actually, still water doesn't do much damage. But as soon as water starts to move, everything changes. To feel this for yourself, turn on your bathroom tap and place your hand underneath.

As **gravity** tugs on the water in mountain streams, the water picks up speed. The faster the water moves, the more force it has. Also, the faster a stream moves, the more **sediments** it can hold. In fact, if a stream's speed doubles, it can carry four times more material.

Eventually, the stream empties into a larger river. When a river's raging waters empty into the sea, they suddenly encounter strong ocean currents moving in different directions. The river water slows down and all its sediments drop down to the ocean floor. The Mississippi River dumps about 220 million tons of new sediments into the Gulf of Mexico every year (above).

If you look at a photo of the Mississippi River taken from space, you can see all the sediments. You can also see how the buildup of sediment blocks the river, causing the water to fork out in many directions and form a **delta.**

How Sedimentary Rock Forms

Sedimentary rock forms slowly over millions of years as sediments slowly build up, compact, and harden. Then **erosion,** earthquakes, or other natural forces may lift or shift the layers so they rise to the surface.

Each year, rivers dump tons of sand, mud, and tiny pebbles into Earth's oceans. As microscopic sea creatures die, their tiny skeletons and shells also fall to the ocean floor. The action of waves sorts all these **sediments** into horizontal layers, or beds. The largest, heaviest materials fall through the water more quickly, so they form the bottom layers. Layers of lighter materials form on top of them.

Over time, these materials build up. The weight of the sediments at the top presses down on the lower layers. All that pressure squeezes out the water and cements the sediments together to form rock. The sediments are glued together by some of the **minerals** from the rocks. If you look closely at sedimentary rock, you may be able to see its layers.

Different kinds of sediments form different kinds of sedimentary rock. For example, sandstone is made mostly of sandy sediments. Smaller particles

SEDIMENTS IN SEDIMENTARY ROCK

SEDIMENTARY ROCK	SEDIMENTS INSIDE
Breccia	A variety of stones and pebbles with sharp edges
Conglomerate	A variety of stones and pebbles with rounded edges
Diatomite	Shells of tiny marine creatures called **diatoms**
Limestone	Shells of marine creatures, especially **foraminifers**
Rock salt	Salt from the ocean
Sandstone	Sand
Shale	Mud or clay

are the main ingredients of siltstone and shale. Most of the shell sediments that make up limestone and diatomite come from animals that are smaller than the head of a pin. Conglomerate and breccia contain a variety of different-sized materials.

Conglomerate is formed when pieces of sedimentary rock become cemented in silica, calcite, or limonite. The pieces can be as small as pebbles or as large as boulders.

SEE FOR YOURSELF

To find out how wave action sorts rocky material by size and weight, add a few spoonfuls of pebbles, sand, and soil to a large glass jar. Then fill the jar with water, screw on the lid tightly, grasp the jar with both hands, and shake it up. Place the jar on a flat surface and let the sediments settle overnight. The next morning, you should see that the sediments have arranged themselves in layers, or beds. The largest and heaviest materials should be on the bottom of the jar, while the smaller, most lightweight materials should make up the top layer.

Sedimentary Stories

The Grand Canyon is an amazing example of how rock layers form over time. The Colorado River began carving the canyon about six million years ago, but scientists think that the rock layers at the bottom may be a billion years old!

Sedimentary rock tells a story about how and when it formed, and what weather conditions were like at the time. For example, ripples in sandstone show which way the wind was blowing or the water was moving when the materials were deposited. If you look closely at rock formations in Zion National Park in southwestern Utah, you can see how drifting sand dunes shifted over time as winds changed.

The Grand Canyon formed over millions of years as the Colorado River **eroded** layer after layer of sedimentary rock—more than 6,560 feet (2,000 meters) of rock in all. More than twenty different layers of sandstone and other kinds of sedimentary rock can be seen in the walls of the Grand Canyon. By studying the canyon's colorful walls, scientists can find clues about how the temperature and climate of the area has changed over time.

Many sedimentary rocks contain **fossils.** Fossils are the remains of plants, animals, and other living things. Ancient animal tracks and trails, eggs, and nests are also fossils.

Plants and animals die all the time, but most do not become fossils. Fossils are rare because conditions must be just right for them to form. Body parts can become fossils only if a dead creature falls into the water or is buried quickly by **sediments.** Otherwise, the corpse will be eaten by animals or rot because it is exposed to air.

At one time, this fossil of a fish was buried deep underground. As the land changed over time, it eventually came to the surface.

Most sedimentary rock forms in shallow seas near the continents. That's why fossils of sea creatures are quite common. Sediments may also build up on lake beds, in deserts, along river valleys, or at the foot of large mountain ranges.

Each fossil find can help scientists learn about an ancient creature and its habitat. By studying many fossils, paleontologists—scientists who study prehistoric life by examining fossils—can piece together how life on Earth has **evolved** and how Earth has changed over time.

DID YOU KNOW?

Long ago, people had no idea what fossils were or how they formed. Some people claimed mammoth tusks were horns from unicorns. Others believed fossils of ancient sea creatures called ammonites were coiled snakes that had been turned to stone by a powerful enchantress. A few even thought the fossils of oyster shells were the devil's toenails.

Where on Earth Is Sedimentary Rock?

No matter where in the world you go, it's easy to find sedimentary rock. It is on Earth's surface now because, over time, ancient seas have disappeared and forces inside Earth have lifted the land.

The Yorkshire Dales of England feature many limestone cliffs and caves. The sedimentary layers were laid down about 300 million years ago, and were exposed as glaciers moved over the land during the Ice Ages.

The Rock of Gibraltar, located near the southern tip of Spain, is made of limestone. So are the Yorkshire Dales in northern England and an area in China called the Stone Forest.

Ayers Rock may be the most famous natural sedimentary structure in the world. Located in the Australian outback, this red sandstone

DID YOU KNOW?

About 100 million years ago, an ancient sea covered much of what we now call the Great Plains of North America. The alternating layers of mudstone and sandstone that make up Capitol Reef National Park in Utah formed as the shoreline of the ancient sea receded, or withdrew.

formation rises 1,140 feet (348 meters) above the desert floor and is about 5.9 miles (9.5 kilometers) wide. Scientists believe that at least two-thirds of the giant rock is still underground. Aborigines, Australia's native people, still call Ayers Rock *Uluru*. They believe it is a sacred place, and have painted animals and scenes on the walls of **caves** within the formation.

Beautiful **travertine** terraces drape the land in an area of Turkey known as Pamukkale Falls. In Yellowstone National Park, a travertine structure known as Minerva Terrace looks like a frozen waterfall. Believe it or not, the rocky structure grows and changes almost as quickly as a real waterfall. A layer of travertine about 12 inches (30 centimeters) thick is added to Minerva Terrace each year.

No water flows over Pamukkale Falls in Turkey. The "falls" are made of travertine, a **mineral** deposited by water from hot and cold springs.

At Petrified Forest National Park in Arizona, large tepee-shaped hills of sandstone and siltstone show signs of thousands of years of **erosion.** The nearby Painted Desert has more than a dozen colorful layers of limestone, sandstone, and shale.

A ROCKY LIFE

The creatures that make up limestone and diatomite are still common on Earth today, but they are so small that you need a microscope to see them. **Foraminifers** and **diatoms** are neither plants nor animals. They belong to a group of living things called **protists.**

A Look at Caves

What can be as small as a telephone booth or as large as a mountain? A **cave**—a natural opening in the ground that is large enough to hold a person.

Most caves form when water slowly eats away at sedimentary rock, such as limestone. As water flows through the ground, it picks up bits of carbon dioxide and forms a weak acid. When the water seeps through cracks between layers of limestone, the rock slowly dissolves. Over time, the cracks grow wider and deeper. Eventually, large caverns and passages form. Years later, the land is lifted up, most of the water drains out, and the passages fill with air.

Deep inside most limestone caves, **mineral**-rich waters drip off the ceilings and flow along the floors.

Caves form slowly as water dissolves soft sedimentary rock (center of illustration). After creating sink-holes at the surface, the water trickles downward and wears away the weakest layers (at right of illustration).

When that water **evaporates,** a kind of limestone called **travertine** is left behind. Giant travertine structures form in some caves. Thin, icicle-shaped stalactites grow down from the ceiling, while stubby stalagmites grow up from the floor. Sometimes stalactites and stalagmites meet and form thick columns.

Other beautiful stone structures may cover the walls. Some are shaped like flowers, bubbles, or pearls, while others look similar to chunks of coral or twisted strands of hair. These delicate features are usually white or gray, but they may be pink, orange, yellow, or even blue. Their color depends on the minerals that make up the sedimentary rock.

Ingleborough Cave in Yorkshire, England, features dozens of beautiful stalactites and stalagmites. The colors are created by impurities in the minerals that formed the structures.

How People Use Sedimentary Rock

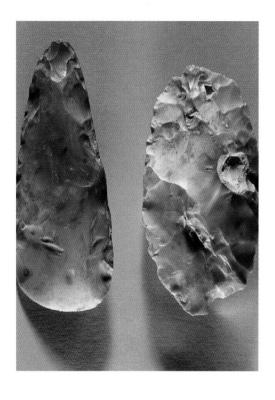

Thousands of years ago, some people used a sedimentary rock called flint to make tools. Flint is easy to break, and it has sharp edges. It was perfect for making axes to cut down trees, knives to skin animals, and shovels to dig out canoes. When ancient peoples rubbed two pieces of flint together, the resulting spark could be used to start fires. The world's first firearms depended on flint for the sparks that ignited gunpowder.

These flint tools were used by people who lived on Earth thousands of years ago. You can see where the rock was chipped away to make sharp edges.

DID YOU KNOW?

People living near the spot where the Niagara River crosses the United States–Canadian border can enjoy the spectacular beauty of Niagara Falls any time. But they also depend on the falls for electricity and for money from the tourist trade.

Niagara Falls consists of two waterfalls—the Horseshoe Falls and the American Falls. Both formed when the river was unable to wear down an 80-foot (24-meter)-thick layer of hard rock but could break up the softer sedimentary layers a little farther downstream.

Today we make windowpanes, dishes, and eyeglasses from ground sandstone or limestone. These rocks are heated with other materials until they melt. When the mixture cools, it is clear enough to see through. Ground limestone is sometimes added to paper and toothpaste. The ground rock gives these products their white color.

Rock salt is a sedimentary rock that is mined from large underground beds that formed when ancient seas evaporated. We use ground-up rock salt to preserve and add flavor to the food we eat.

You probably can't imagine eating sedimentary rocks, but they make your french fries taste better. Table salt is ground-up rock salt, and rock salt is a sedimentary rock. Rock salt comes from mines all over the world. It formed when ancient seas **evaporated,** leaving all their salt behind. As time passed, other **sediments** buried the salty sediments deep under the ground.

THE VALUE OF FLINT

Christina Rossetti (1830–1894) was a well-known British poet. She wrote the following poem about flint.

An emerald is green as grass;
A ruby red as blood;
A sapphire shines blue as heaven;
A flint lies in the mud.

A diamond is a brilliant stone,
To catch the world's desire.
An opal holds a fiery spark;
But only flint holds fire.

Sedimentary Structures

The Pyramid of Kukulkan in Chichen Itza, Mexico, is made of limestone. It was built by the Maya about 1,000 years ago.

Limestone has been a popular building material for thousands of years. It is attractive, readily available, and easy to work with. The ancient Egyptians used it to build great pyramids that rose taller than a forty-story skyscraper. The ancient Maya also constructed impressive pyramids from limestone. One of these structures, the Pyramid of Kukulkan, still stands today in Chichen Itza on the Yucatán Peninsula in Mexico.

Nôtre Dame, a famous cathedral in Paris, France, is also made of limestone. So is St. Paul's Cathedral in London, England. Today, builders use limestone blocks to construct many public buildings, such as schools and libraries.

Limestone is not the only popular sedimentary building material. Polished breccia was used to build some parts of the Opera House in Paris, France, and the Pantheon in Rome, Italy.

The ancient Egyptians used sandstone, another sedimentary rock, to create the Great Sphinx more than 4,500 years ago. This huge statue, with the head of a man and the body of a lion, may have been modeled after a ruler buried in a nearby pyramid. Some modern public buildings, such as courthouses and town halls, have also been built with sandstone blocks. The "brownstones" that line the streets of many large cities are buildings made of red sandstone.

ANCIENT ARCHITECTS

Cement is made of limestone that has been ground and heated. When sand, gravel, and water are added to cement, we call it concrete. Concrete was invented by the ancient Egyptians, but it was improved tremendously by the Romans.

The ancient Romans were expert architects and builders. They constructed great arenas, such as the Colosseum (above); impressive bridges, such as the Pont du Gard; and extraordinary temples, such as the Pantheon. All of these structures are made of a mixture of concrete and brick that has been covered with more attractive rock.

The Rock Cycle

Over millions of years, waves and ocean currents have carved these structures, called the Twelve Apostles, along the coast of Australia. The giant pillars are made of limestone.

Rocks are always changing. Forces deep underground and on Earth's surface destroy some rocks and, at the same time, create new ones. But the process takes place so slowly that we often don't even notice it.

Erosion and **weathering** slowly break down even the hardest rocks on Earth. The tiny rocky bits are picked up by streams and rivers. Each day, rivers dump tons of **sediments** into Earth's oceans. At the same time, ocean currents and waves also wear down rocky coastlines. Over thousands of years, sediments build up. As the weight of the upper layers presses down on materials below, the rock compacts and sticks together to form giant beds of sedimentary rock.

As Earth's **plates** move, some of the sedimentary rock is twisted and folded. When the **minerals** in the rock break down or change, **metamorphic rock** forms. Shifting plates pull other regions of sedimentary rock into the **mantle,** where the rock melts and becomes **magma.** Eventually, some of the magma spills onto the land and cools to form **igneous rock.** Pools of magma also become trapped where the **crust** and mantle meet. As it cools, it too becomes igneous rock.

As even more time passes, the new igneous and metamorphic rocks also break down and wear away. Eventually, they too will be carried back to the ocean and form new layers of sedimentary rock. The result is a never-ending process—all the minerals that make up Earth's rock are continually recycled as the rocks themselves are created and destroyed.

Melting to reform magma

Heat and pressure

Metamorphic Rock

Igneous Rock

Heat and pressure

Erosion and build up of sediment

Melting to reform magma

Erosion and build up of sediment

Sedimentary Rock

Erosion and build up of sediment

The rock we see on Earth today has not always been here. Rock forms and breaks down in a never-ending cycle.

DID YOU KNOW?

Wear and tear from the wind and waves has formed natural bridges, rock arches, and **blow holes** in many parts of the world. At Arches National Park in Utah (right), impressive sandstone formations crisscross the land. One well-known blow hole is found on Hook Island, one of the Galápagos Islands off the shore of Ecuador. It is called Nature's Toilet because the water flowing in and out looks similar to water in a flushing toilet.

Is That a Sedimentary Rock?

Colorful rock layers in Arizona's Painted Desert suggest that they are made of sedimentary rock. The rock was lifted to the surface millions of years ago and has been **eroded** by wind and water ever since.

Petrologists can identify a rock by studying its **minerals** closely. Are the minerals hard or soft? Are they shiny or dull? Are their **crystals** large or small?

Luckily, you do not need to know as much as a petrologist does to decide whether a rock is sedimentary, **igneous,** or **metamorphic.** All you need is a little bit of information about the area where the rock was found. For example, if your hometown was once covered by an ancient sea or lake, you are likely to find plenty of sedimentary rocks in your neighborhood.

Next, think about how sedimentary rock forms, and ask yourself some questions about your rock sample. Does it have colorful layers? Can you see fragments of pebbles or shells in the rock? Are there ripple marks? Does the rock contain any **fossils?** If the answer to one or more of these questions is "yes," you probably have a sedimentary rock. In addition, many sedimentary rocks are soft. So if you can break a rock with your hands, there's a good chance it's a sedimentary rock.

You may also want to take a quick look at the minerals. The minerals that make up most sedimentary rock are soft and dull with small crystals.

Of course, one of the best ways to identify a rock is to study a field guide to rocks and minerals. These books show pictures of rocks and give detailed descriptions of them.

A TELLTALE TEST

If you think you've found limestone, try a simple test. Pour some warm soda pop over the rock. If it fizzes like crazy, it's limestone. The chemicals in the soda pop react with the minerals that make up limestone. This chemical reaction breaks down the limestone, so you shouldn't try it on a limestone building.

IN SEARCH OF SHALE

Learning to identify shale can really pay off. This soft, gray sedimentary rock often contains oil deposits. Oil is the remains of tiny ocean plants and animals called **plankton**. When plankton die, their bodies sink to the bottom of the ocean and are buried by **sediments**. As time passes, the plankton turn into a thick, black liquid, and most of the sediments turn into shale.

Be a Rock Hound

These young rock hounds are finding rock samples during a class trip to a local creek bed. Do you think they are examining a sedimentary rock?

DID YOU KNOW?

A geologist is a scientist who studies rocks and rock formations to learn how Earth formed and how it has changed over time. Florence Bascom (1862–1945) was the first American woman to become a professional geologist.

Now that you know how to spot sedimentary rocks, would you like to collect some? You can buy all kinds of beautiful and interesting sedimentary rock samples. You can also see them at a natural history museum, but it might be more fun to hunt for your own rocks at a local park, in a field, or in the woods.

Before you begin planning your first rock hunting trip, you will need to gather a few pieces of equipment. You will also need to learn a few rules.

Once you have identified the rocks, you may want to create a system for labeling, organizing, and storing them. Then you will always be able to find

a specific sample when you need it. You can arrange your specimens any way you like—by color, by **crystal** shape, by collection site, or even alphabetically. As your collection grows, being organized will become more and more important.

There are many ways to organize a rock collection. You can use a box with dividers or glue specimens to a piece of cardboard.

WHAT YOU NEED

- Hiking boots
- A map and compass
- A pick and rock hammer to collect samples
- Safety glasses to keep rock chips out of your eyes
- A small paintbrush to remove dirt and extra rock chips from samples
- A camera to take photographs of rock formations
- A hand lens to get an up-close look at **minerals**
- A notebook for recording when and where you find each rock
- A field guide to rocks and minerals

WHAT YOU NEED TO KNOW

- Never go rock hunting alone. Go with a group that includes an adult.
- Know how to read a map and use a compass.
- Always get a landowner's permission before walking on private property. If you find interesting rocks, ask the owner if you may remove them.
- Before removing samples from public land, make sure collecting is allowed. Many natural rock formations are protected by law.
- Respect nature. Do not disturb living things, and do not litter.

Glossary

acid rain: rain that is polluted with acid in the atmosphere and that damages the environment

atom: smallest unit of an element that has all of the properties of that element

blow hole: opening in a rock formation created by wind erosion

cave: natural opening in the ground that is large enough to hold a person

core: center of Earth. The inner core is solid, and the outer core is liquid.

crust: outer layer of Earth

crystal: repeating structural unit within most minerals

delta: formation of deposits that a river dumps at the spot where it empties into the ocean

diatom: one-celled sea creature that may live alone or cluster with other diatoms. Some diatoms are round; others are long and thin.

erode: to slowly wear away rock over time by the action of wind, water, or glaciers

evaporate: to change from a liquid to a gas

evolved: changed slowly; adapted to changing environmental conditions

face: smooth, flat side of a crystal

foraminifer: one-celled sea creature with a simple shell

fossil: remains or evidence of ancient life

gravity: force that pulls objects toward Earth's center

igneous rock: kind of rock that forms when magma from Earth's mantle cools and hardens

magma: hot, soft rock that makes up Earth's mantle. When magma spills out onto the surface, it is called lava.

mantle: layer of Earth between the crust and outer core. It is made of soft rock called magma.

metamorphic rock: kind of rock that forms when heat or pressure changes the minerals within igneous rock, sedimentary rock, or another metamorphic rock

mineral: natural solid material with a specific chemical makeup and structure

plankton: tiny creatures that float on top of the water. Plankton is an important source of food for fish and other sea animals.

plate: one of the large slabs of rock that make up Earth's crust

property: trait or characteristic that helps make identification possible

protist: tiny, simple creature. All plants, animals, and fungi evolved from protists.

sediment: mud, clay, or bits of rock picked up by rivers and streams and dumped in the ocean

travertine: mineral consisting of massive layered calcium carbonate

volcano: crack in Earth's surface that extends into the mantle, and from which comes melted rock

weathering: breaking down of rock by plant roots or by repeated freezing and thawing

To Find Out More

BOOKS

Blobaum, Cindy. *Geology Rocks!: 50 Hands-On Activities to Explore the Earth.* Charlotte, Vt.: Williamson, 1999.

Christian, Peggy. *If You Find a Rock.* New York: Harcourt Brace, 2000.

Gallant, Roy A. *Limestone Caves.* Danbury, Conn.: Franklin Watts, 1998.

Hiscock, Bruce. *The Big Rock.* New York: Aladdin, 1999.

Hopper, Merredith. *The Pebble in My Pocket: A History of Our Earth.* New York: Viking, 1994.

Kittinger, Jo S. *A Look at Rocks: From Coal to Kimberlite.* Danbury, Conn.: Franklin Watts, 1997.

Oldershaw, Cally. *3D-Eyewitness: Rocks and Minerals.* New York: Dorling Kindersley, 1999.

Pellant, Chris. *The Best Book of Fossils, Rocks, and Minerals.* New York: Kingfisher, 2000.

Ricciuti, Edward, and Margaret W. Carruthers. *National Audubon Society First Field Guide to Rocks and Minerals.* New York: Scholastic, 1998.

Staedter, Tracy. *Rocks and Minerals.* Pleasantville, N.Y.: Reader's Digest, 1999.

ORGANIZATIONS

Geological Survey of Canada
601 Booth Street
Ottawa, Ontario
KIA 0E8
613/995-3084

U.S. Geological Survey (USGS)
507 National Center
12201 Sunrise Valley Drive
Reston, VA 22092
703/648-4748

Index